# BEING AN ENTREPRENEUR

## A SIMPLE GUIDE TO
## BEING A GREAT INNOVATOR

CRAIG A. BARNETT

authorHOUSE®

*AuthorHouse*™
*1663 Liberty Drive*
*Bloomington, IN 47403*
*www.authorhouse.com*
*Phone: 1 (800) 839-8640*

*Published by AuthorHouse   01/08/2018*

*ISBN: 978-1-5246-9457-9 (sc)*
*ISBN: 978-1-5246-9455-5 (hc)*
*ISBN: 978-1-5246-9456-2 (e)*

*Library of Congress Control Number: 2017908561*

*Print information available on the last page.*

# Contents

# Don't Be Afraid

So, you woke up in the middle of the night or from a vivid daydream on the bus and realized that you have a great idea for a product. Don't be afraid. This book will give you the skills and tools to confidently convert your idea into reality! Sometimes being unafraid is easier said than done. Indeed, the fear of failure is what keeps most entrepreneurs from achieving their goals and bringing their ideas to life. Some common things you will read or hear about successful entrepreneurs is that they acknowledged and were able to manage their fear of failure and use it to their advantage. Still, many fantastic ideas and inventions have never made it into mainstream markets because the inventors, or those around them, slowed down the process and kept things from moving forward.

In this book, I will refer to a "project," meaning the full lifecycle of an original product or service—from idea to completion. Thinking about your idea as a project encourages you to set goals and keep a holistic view of your progress. It gives you the ability to set milestones and build a roadmap that includes the high-level tasks needed to complete the project. Here, for example, is a simple project timeline:

- Month 1 to 3. Develop an idea.
- Months 4 to 6. Research current viability and uses.
- Months 7 to 8. Create a solid business plan.
- Months 9 to 12. Convene a trusted group of consultants.
- Months 13 to 15. Define the business tasks required.
- Months 16 to 24. Execute your idea.

I will also highlight examples of the types of toxic individuals and elements in your environment that can influence the overall outcome. As your project moves through its lifecycle, these elements may produce an aura of fear that confuses the process and prevents the project from reaching its full potential. Always take full ownership of your ideas and projects, remain the sole final decision maker until the project becomes a product or service. The ultimate litmus test will come when you sell your creation to the broader community and the all-important and (sometimes) judgmental consumer.

First, let's discuss fear of failure. Everyone fails at something from time to time, and it is well documented that learning from one's mistakes establishes a stronger sense of stability and reality. It is easy for people to boast about success and talk at length about their own shortcomings and failures, especially if they have already experienced, and conquered, what you are about to go through. Sometimes failure doesn't have quite the same impact on newly energized entrepreneurs, because all we want to do is be successful. However, what we need to do—now and not a moment later—is escape the strong inner desire to succeed.

Failure is an important part of progress because it teaches us what *not* to do next time and helps us build the methods we use to develop new ideas and kick-start projects. Entrepreneurs dislike failure but will eventually learn to accept it. Some will give up altogether, deciding that it is just too hard. But you should welcome failure as learning, *not* an excuse to escape from the powerful internal determination that will bring your ideas to life.

Timing is also important when you are seeking to bring a new product or service to the world. I have seen entrepreneurs who appear to be flogging a dead horse; somehow, they find a way to make it look like there's life in the old mustang yet. These people have spent too long on their ideas and possibly need to place them on the back burner. Try not to dedicate too many resources to an idea that doesn't have strong traction. Try to do this without listening to others who are critical of your project, and don't consider yourself succumbing to fear. At this point, simply accept that the idea needs to grow a little further. I will provide some techniques for how to do this later in this book.

Once you curb the fear of failure, you will find a new ability to nurture your ideas. When you understand and are aware of fear, it can no longer affect you or hold you back. Just acknowledge the fear—that it exists and is real. Then watch as it loses its influence over you during your entrepreneurial journey. It's liberating to willingly confront fear and use the experience to jump over hurdles. There will be many opportunities for you to turn back fear as you continue on your journey. It becomes easier over time.

Using your own intuition and the feedback from your trusted group of advisors, which you will identify shortly, you will see the potential of the opportunity, and maybe steps you had not taken into account will become clearer along the way. Once fear has been set aside, at least for the time being, you can identify credible roadblocks that might cause hiccups but won't cripple your idea. Always keep a positive frame of mind, remembering that you can slightly alter your ideas to bypass hurdles; this can give you a vision to completion. Although feedback is important, it will ultimately only highlight others' opinions and may not be entirely accurate. Still, don't be afraid to ask for honest feedback at each and every step of the way. If people sense you cannot take constructive feedback well, they may hold back key information. The feedback you do receive may tell you whether you should fail fast or carry on. *Failing fast* means identifying that nothing is working as it should and stopping the project as quickly as possible, avoiding the loss of unnecessary funds and time. Despite all the feedback you receive and no matter how much information you obtain on the Internet or from any other informational reservoir, the buck stops with you!

Sit in a comfortable environment, and collate the information you have. Ensure all decisions are yours, not something conjured up by fear-mongers. As I mentioned earlier, it's always rewarding to talk with successful people who describe how they almost failed but managed to push through by removing roadblocks one at a time, sharing their stories on a global scale. If you decide to close down your project, take comfort in the knowledge that you have learned from the experience, which will benefit your next idea and the idea after that.

Secondly, fear of moving ahead on an idea because of someone else's opinion should never slow down or influence completion of the project. Fear is the other person's responsibility, not yours, so do not entertain the concept of absorbing it on his or her behalf. There are enough challenges within your control on which to focus. A simple tool to use is a journal; update it regularly, maintain a running list of activities, and reflect on them. List the hurdles you overcame to get beyond the blocks, when fear was involved and when it wasn't, and document the outcomes. Achieve this, and you will be on your way from a new idea to project completion.

Consider the potential outcome of lack of movement and action. While fear has the potential to leave smart people paralyzed and unable to complete their projects, it also builds up over time until you believe the ultimate lie: "I can't do this or anything else." Of course, only a brief look around will show you that many entrepreneurs have been successfully innovative in the past and present, and many will be successful in our future. Everything you see was invented at some point. Imagine the frustration of some of these inventors when their ideas initially didn't work. They didn't give up, which is why we are surrounded by so many intuitive and interesting inventions, some that entertain us and some that sustain life.

However, some people just don't get it. For many individuals, seeing beyond what is in front of them is an impossible and daunting task. Some people never ask themselves, "How did that get there? Did someone invent that?"

I ask myself those questions each day. It's fun seeing an invention as it is today and thinking about how complex or simple it would have been to bring the project to life. Was it completed in a year or two years? Or maybe it took many years to evolve, like mainstream television production companies, who continues to be in high demand and over time has grown into a global market leader. It's a fun way to put things into perspective and gain a little piece of inspiration to get started. By reading this book, you are already flagging yourself as an entrepreneur, and hopefully you can see that most other people will be behind the eight ball when it comes to nurturing good ideas.

We have focused on the risks associated with fear and some of the hurdles. Now, let's talk about some simple thought tools, which we already have at our disposal, and learn how to use them effectively, which will help us finish what we started:

- Inventions exist all around us, so they must be a possibility and not a pipe dream.
- Others walked this path before I did, and others will do so afterward.
- People who are afraid all the time do not achieve their goals
- Being afraid is for other people, not us
- The greatest words in the arsenal of an entrepreneur who is being challenged: "What have *you* created lately?"

The last point in the above list was my greatest tool when I was developing projects. It was a simple statement that I would either direct to someone who was challenging my ideas or myself, or if I had sat on a project for far too long. For some entrepreneurs, standing still for more than a day can cause frustration and a sense of being late. This feeling of being late has motivated me many times. In fact, writing this book came from the fact that I hadn't completed any projects in a few months and I thought I should get moving. Filling the gap with something creative, such as writing, is an easy way to get your ideas across to anyone willing to listen, and inspire the creative part of your mind to move new ideas from the back burner to the forefront.

Over time, you will come up with some thought tools of your own. They can be anything that motivates you or helps you identify when others are projecting their own anxiety onto you. Often others are jealous or afraid of people who are on an innovation journey. Consider watching how others react to certain circumstances or events around them.. You will notice that you begin to react differently—perhaps more as a problem solver than someone who walks away. Although the world's population is large, a simple reality remains true: "everyone is different." Accept that as fact. Over time, you will justify your choices and decisions through your project lifecycle, and everything you learn will contribute to your framework for success.

As you continue reading this book, you will learn more tools and tricks to lift your project off the ground. Make notes, and keep a journal along the way to reflect on at a later stage. I have had successful entrepreneurs read this book at the beginning, middle and end of their project lifestyle as a simple reference guide to tell them where they are, and help them plan next steps. This guidebook is just that, an awareness guide of information I have found valuable on my journey.

Always remember that some people are not able to graduate to "being an entrepreneur," but you can!

# What Is an Entrepreneur?

Sometimes I wonder if only non-entrepreneurs can define what an entrepreneur actually is. More than likely, the two groups will disagree.

The obvious place to start is by reiterating that all people are different. There are similar traits in personalities and abilities such as intellectual capacities, problem-solving skills, energy and motivation levels; however, no two people are alike (twins included). From observation, I believe entrepreneurs fall into two categories: the *business entrepreneur* and the *innovator entrepreneur*. Throughout this book, I will remind you that identifying the skills you don't have is a great and admirable talent.

Business entrepreneurs are generally innovators who work with existing solutions in a company's current portfolio of products. They have business skills and are often natural leaders in the workplace. People inside and outside the office will gravitate to them due to their energy and motivation they naturally exude. Business entrepreneurs are deep thinkers and certainly do not waste time or subscribe to gossip, especially during projects with strict delivery timeframes. Often thinking on their feet, their entrepreneurial side will encourage them to make rapid changes or product enhancements without a formal presentation or full sign off. They will always trust themselves to get it right and usually have the knowledge and expertise to do so. Their talent motivates others to get involved and go the extra mile. Sometimes, business entrepreneurs will stay with your company for fifteen years, whether you want them to or not.

Innovator entrepreneurs sit at the other end of the spectrum, although they still have the ability to trust in themselves. These entrepreneurs will most likely work in isolation to discover, invent, create and innovate. They are often highly emotional and share their project ideas with others too early in the creation process. In addition, these entrepreneurs will seek out others who are having difficulty with projects or ideas of their own and actively attempt to solve their problems. This trait is a minor flaw, simply because innovator entrepreneurs are motivated to solve problems that others cannot. Often, that help will go unrewarded and may propel someone else's project forward faster than expected. After the problem has been solved, the innovator entrepreneur will walk away buoyant, with a sense of achievement. And although the person who was helped most likely will sleep easily that night, they will not give the entrepreneur any financial reward.

Be very cautious about the people you help. They often will do one of two things. They will vanish into the night, and you may never hear from them again. Or they will strike up a false friendship, thinking of you as their own personal safety blanket, striving to have you work for free. You might say, "That won't happen to me," but chances are, it already has.

Innovator entrepreneurs enjoy spending time on their own; however, sometimes, this creates an environment of isolation, and they are often labeled as a recluse. They most likely still go to work, embracing a high workload and disproportionately low salary, lacking the confidence to discuss roles and responsibilities or salary increases with management. When moonlighting as inventors, they grow in motivation and achieve satisfying feelings of euphoria. This probably is a good time to mention that illegal drugs and alcohol inhibit innovation; keep your feet on the ground and remain focused. The urge to create the success in your mind and live out your dreams before you finish the project can be quite potent. It can lead to an exaggerated lifestyle as you attempt to reflect success that hasn't yet come to fruition, projecting an unlikely and improbable outcome. The urge to think too far into the future will slow down the innovation and invention process. The desire to move your recently conceived idea into mainstream distribution in one month is highly addictive and most likely impossible.

Our basic genetic makeup is to be social animals, and the default response of immediately trusting everyone only affords people the opportunity to break your trust. Therefore, the default response is inherently flawed. It will slow production, delay the go-to-market strategy, and place your project at risk.

I apologize for focusing more on the innovator entrepreneur; however, this personality type is more likely to fail due to high emotion and internalized frustration. In the past, I've been warned about the concept of misplaced trust. Perhaps you have too. Instead, trust no one in the beginning, and rely on  others only when they've earned your trust. While we all have an urge to connect with others, find your balance and remain consistent.

Strangely enough, both types of entrepreneur—business and innovator—have a self-motivating sense of freedom. They are often happy with the basic necessities in life and don't want to become responsible for changing the status quo. Of course, that is before they launch a new product that can potentially disrupt the marketplace; then it simply becomes fun. The recluse in most innovator entrepreneurs may slow this process demonstrably; they may say, "There is always tomorrow." This should be a red flag that identifies that momentum has slowed or stopped.

A tool to use, in this situation and others that slow your progress, is a fantastic saying by Mark Twain: "Eat your frog first thing in the morning, and that will probably be the worst thing you do all day." It is terrible to think about eating a frog; however, if you have to eat it eventually, you may as well get it over and done with first thing in the morning, so it won't be on your mind all day. If you have an important but challenging task that you have put off for some time, chances are this is your frog. Complete that task—whether it is a phone call, document, job application, or resignation—first thing in the morning. Then stop thinking about it for the rest of the day; now that the toughest task on your list has been addressed, you can move onto the next one. Eventually, you will notice that the difficulty in your tasks plateau at a manageable level, making day-to-day activities easier.

This wonderfully motivating statement from Mark Twain helps keep momentum going, and I often use it to help me tackle the day's tasks. For example, I find that I can handle nine tasks slowly; however, the tenth seems to break the camel's back and stall all progression. When I face a particularly daunting or difficult task, and put my fresh mind to its completion first thing in the morning, I feel more confident about getting through the workload in front of me. In some circumstances, it has motivated me to address more challenging tasks throughout the day.

During your journey to define what being an entrepreneur means to you, and at which end of the spectrum you reside, think about areas that are not your core competencies. That is how entrepreneurs differentiate between tasks that they are capable of completing but have a block in addressing those things that need to be handled urgently but require experience and knowledge outside their arsenal of skills. At these times, external resources become very valuable. For example, I am not an accountant; therefore, I do not complete my own tax returns. I have a trusted accountant who helps me with financial management and company growth/creation. I am not a solicitor either, so I don't write my own wills, give advice on the legality of circumstances, and I certainly wouldn't represent myself in a court of law. These legal and accounting resources are a critical part of my corporate team and will be so on every new project. It's important to develop these relationships during the "trusting" phase of your journey, and remain engaged while the relationship grows into one of trust. We will discuss these resources further in upcoming chapters.

Depending on your view of the type of entrepreneur you are or will become, accept that everyone sees things in a very different light. People become frustrated for many reasons. On your journey you will notice that some people will have absolutely no idea what you are trying to create. When these people become frustrated, they criticize and try to dismantle the benefits of your project outcomes. Remember to take their criticism like a grain of salt. If they don't understand your idea for any reason, let them go. They don't want to be part of a conversation on subject matter they know nothing about. Projects that typically cause this type of reaction are application development, Internet concepts, anything financial or technical, or any subject that is beyond their experience. Don't feel bad about the responses you get, and do not let them affect your self-esteem. If no one understands you, then you might just have a unique idea.

There are also blends of the two entrepreneur types discussed above. There is a sliding scale between working hard as a leader and becoming a complete recluse. Both types of entrepreneur are capable of innovation and invention. Once you identify where you sit on the entrepreneur sliding scale, you can use that knowledge, and your idea, to find gaps in the global marketplace. Every industry has gaps, which will present themselves to those who look closely enough. For example, the iPod was a globally disruptive innovation that filled a gap in the marketplace. People have always wanted to listen to music when walking or jogging. The gap was the reliance on cassettes and other mediums. Apple invented the iPod to do not only digitize music, but also to back it up safely, replicate it to other devices, and access a central store to purchase individual songs, instead of an entire album on a flaky and unreliable magnetic medium. An idea manifested itself to solve a problem, then enhanced to differentiate itself in all marketplaces.

Knowing which type of entrepreneur you are gives you the ability to start the innovation process properly. A great place to start is to research likeminded individuals who have gone before you. Knowledge about their individual journeys will comfort you about success, frighten you about failure, and make you think your idea just might be possible. The world needs and craves new innovation in the marketplace. Our society is built mostly of people who are happy to pay for new products but never want to be involved in their development.

Whether you want to disrupt the marketplace or create a market tipping point, meaning the point at which more consumers are purchasing your product versus any competitors, you need to have the guts to give it a go. One part of this journey that I found most rewarding was observing my own transitions. With the knowledge you gain from this book and other resources, over time your position on the entrepreneur sliding scale will shift. My hope is that both extremes of the spectrum learn from each other, ultimately meeting somewhere in the middle. Understanding what you have and have not done well is the only way to move your skill set toward that point.

Once the recluses, i.e., the innovator entrepreneurs, build confidence and knowledge, they will shift toward the middle. This could be a long process; however, they will feel the difference when it begins to happen. Remember, when I said I wasn't an accountant? That's true; however, over time, I have learned skills in money management, budgets, and balance sheets—moving ever so slightly toward the middle.

Once the business entrepreneurs build confidence in technology and learn skills outside their normal comfort zones, they too will shift toward the middle of the scale. These changes won't affect major skills; they merely highlight an insight into knowledge you otherwise didn't have. Remember, when I said I wasn't a solicitor? That's still true; however, along the way I learned a great deal about company constitutions, trademarks and patents, and confidentiality agreements, which I can now read with understanding when I receive them from other companies.

Ultimately, the definition of an entrepreneur is what you perceive it to be, which will motivate you to complete your project. Often, this will be connected to your moral compass, basic ethics, and overall view about changing the world with one idea. The next few chapters will identify tools and processes to help you move through the project lifecycle. A critical thing is to rapidly identify what you are not good at. The entrepreneur personality has a distinct "I can do this myself" attitude; unfortunately, that isn't true. Identify your weaknesses and strengths early in the project, because later you will need the confidence to identify what you are not good at over and over again. Connect with trusted resources to help you along the path to success; it will make the entire process easier. Make mistakes, and "eat your frog in the morning."

# Different or Misunderstood

Are entrepreneurs different or misunderstood? Well, we don't live in a world of absolutes, so perhaps they are a bit of both. If we are honest with ourselves, the entire population could fall into either category or even shift seamlessly from one to the other and back again. Everyone at one point is considered different and then misunderstood two breaths later. These two frames of mind are great, broad-spectrum words that capture everyone all at once. Entrepreneurs too can be placed roughly into these two different personality profiles;

**Innovator and Business Entrepreneurs**

These two types obviously can coexist, overlap, and achieve great things on their own while still finding the time to moonlight as budding innovators on the side. Sleep is not a luxury at this stage; rather, it is an unwanted distraction that prevents them from moving faster in their never-ending pursuit of problem-solving inventions. If the two types could work tirelessly with one another, while existing on either side of the entrepreneurial spectrum, I honestly am not sure what would be invented, but I hope I'm around to see it.

Often inventor entrepreneurs are considered fundamental change agents within organizations. Once entrepreneurs are inside a company, they are rapidly identified as idea people and the go-to people if you want something done. Inventor entrepreneurs will operate at the functional levels of an organization where products are changed and improved. They may not be aware, but managers have their eyes on such people, who may come up with a change that further differentiates a product in the marketplace. Business entrepreneurs most likely will be a part of the management team, devising new ways to sell the product and showing constant progress. They will find comfort in the fact that they can operate at both the tactical and the product-development lifecycles, adding value to both.

An entrepreneur respects the rules but often operates outside the rules, considering that to be their comfort zone. Other employees will find this type of entrepreneur to be a little different. Strict policy-driven employees will see an entrepreneur as a major risk and highlight the danger of his or her suggested ideas, which are meant to bring about change. These people are stuck in their ways and fear change immensely; change in the status quo forces them to work more actively on projects and constantly update their skills. It is not uncommon for entrepreneurs to distant themselves from the current operational methods of the business; choosing instead to focus on the products portfolio they want changed, technology or functional enhancements, and sales results.

Coworkers might not like this ability to stay isolated from the everyday operations, and while they may like the individual, they just don't get what makes him or her tick. Many times, they feel the entrepreneur isn't following or is skirting around management's rules and thus is putting the company at risk. Change can frustrate coworkers.

Good managers see a bright star with an unlimited reservoir of potential. They notice that the entrepreneur operates slightly outside the rules, burning the candle at both ends. This understanding from the upper ranks of the company further frustrate coworkers, who eventually may call a meeting with management to discuss. However, the leadership team may have already picked up on levels of tension and frustration among staff, some of whom may believe that the entrepreneur can get away with anything. Management will listen to the concerns and often try to neutralize them by reassuring staff that everything is functioning well, that a change agent is needed to take the company to the next level, and that the future will be exciting and staff will see a wealth of opportunities in the coming months. Essentially, management will sell the entrepreneur as a method of growth and heightened reward for employees, in the event his or her changes drive revenue in the correct direction.

Here is an interesting piece of information: effective managers will remain grounded and calm as they observe the entrepreneur at work. At times, they too will become slightly frustrated, but they will hide it well. They know that the rewards of having such a problem solver on their team far outweigh the alternative. It's a delicate balance for managers, given that at times they will be seen as defending and promoting the entrepreneur to other staff. They may feel that the window for this energy and growth could be short, as the entrepreneur continues to focus on his or own ideas.

Once that idea starts to form and show substance, entrepreneurs often will balance staying with the company, against moving on to focus on their own goals. After all, without management and coworkers, the process is simpler, and the only rules are defined by the entrepreneur. Thus, during staff meetings, managers will try to convince everyone that the entrepreneur is not different, just misunderstood. Later in life when all is said and done, and the manager has moved on to another organizations, he might say, "Yep, that person was a little different, but I think others misunderstood him or her." In the back of the manager's mind will be the annoying thought that one day the entrepreneur may join their new company.

Note: Often, business entrepreneurs and innovator entrepreneurs don't get along. That is part of the fun, I suppose. Before we move any further, let's discuss why you should start by trusting no one.

# Start by Trusting No One

Trust is something that must be earned by others and should not be given away. Moving forward, please consider trust to be one of your most valuable possessions. How many times have you heard about someone who has misplaced trust in another person? It is one of the easiest traps for an entrepreneur to fall into.

Before you gather resources, you must move from your initial thoughts to a minimum level of presentable data that you can articulate with reasonable accuracy, without giving away your intellectual property. The disappointing truth is that we live in a selfish world inhabited with falsehoods and difficult challenges. Friends come thick and fast if they believe they can gain something from your success. Do not be fooled or misled; sometimes these people work in groups to capture your friendship. It is a definite challenge to live in a digitally connected world where social media has taken over general conversation and genuine discussions. People find it easier to communicate, gather resources, and gain your confidence and perhaps access to your finances. Most people understand that money makes the world turn and enables the lifestyle you want for yourself and family. The global markets have an incredible influence on financial security, providing the platform for simple and complex economics, shifting money as the market changes.

How will "trusting no one" help you understand the modern world—social media, the global market, being part of a truly connected society, etc. Well, people are different and also clever. Today's evolutionary version of human instinct determines that the most important agenda item is to get ahead of others at any cost. Money is the unit of measurement that drives those outcomes. Be mindful of what you have, and trust no one, then observe the reactions from those around you. When you act on the "no trusting" strategy, people may connect the dots and believe money is no longer of interest to you and will change their attitude toward you. So start by trusting no one, not even those close to you; sometimes through honest mistakes, even friends and family can jeopardize your project. Find a way to navigate through the minefield of mistrust, keep your purpose at the forefront of your mind, and keep your project secure. It's not time yet, but later in the book we will discuss the negative influence a narcissist can have on your project and life in general; they are a great example of whom not to trust—ever.

If you start by trusting no one, how will your idea progress? The answer will become clearer and simpler over time. Research and document your journey and the project concepts, using whatever documentation strategy works best for you. Information and ideas can be fleeting; keep a journal of your experiences and thoughts relating to the project. Ensure the journal is dedicated solely to the project, and don't mix ideas. Documentation can make or break your project. If you're like me, documentation comes with its fair share of difficulty; however the rewards will be demonstrable.

It's time to identify resources to help you bring your project to a positive end result. You do not have to engage any organizations at this stage, but the roles and responsibilities of others may compliment your idea, and add a tremendous amount of value. Again, do not launch a recruitment drive just yet. The ideal people or roles to engage for your project are people you have not yet met, but can easily research to gauge their market credibility. Examples include an accountant, a technology partner, a business or life management coach, a marketing company and the all-important neutral sounding board.

The resources you choose for external guidance will depend on your current skills as an entrepreneur. For example, a technically capable person may not require much input from an external IT company. If you're a marketing person, perhaps you can complete most of the brand-awareness tasks yourself and use a marketing company as an external check and measure on your strategy. Keep note of the resources you need, and identify three companies that can add value to your idea. Complete credibility checks to ensure the authenticity of the businesses and the viability of their involvement, and solicit bids from like companies to create competition and a palatable fee structure. Once you have a list of resources, ensure your comfort levels are high enough to move to the next stage when the time comes.

As you move through the stage of trusting no one, your documentation will build. It may comprise of drawings and sketches; slowly bringing clarity to your idea and seeing it on paper for the first time is highly rewarding. Your documentation will serve as a point-in-time reference of your ideas journey and serve as evidence to you and others that this is 100% your intellectual property. Thus, your focus needs to be unrelenting when it comes to documentation. To recap, your documentation should include a running journal with time and dates for reference, the beginnings of a timeline linked to the production lifecycle of your idea, and a list of potential resources capable of helping you move to the next stage. Important note: do not put names against the resources you need; instead use the function they will provide. For example, do not write "Bill," the accountant who has completed your tax returns for the last ten years, but rather "a local accountant with credibility."

Relationships will grow depending on the stage of your invention and how quickly you bring resources into the project. The accountant should be the first resource you engage as he or she will highlight areas of personal responsibility and put a legally protective banner across you and your idea. They can assist with patent searches and patent applications, conducted by either his firm or a recommended partner, perhaps a dedicated intellectual property (IP) lawyer. These elements are vital to the protection and credibility of your product. The accountant also will be able to point you to lawyers who can work with you to draft nondisclosure agreements (NDAs) and confidentiality agreements for each entity with which you will work. NDAs and confidentiality agreements do not give you freedom to share your idea with the world; they are simply an IP protection mechanism to keep confidential conversations private, and they act as a good deterrent for those wanting your ideas exploited. Generally speaking, this area is a solicitor's realm of expertise; however,

when your accountant refers you to one or more lawyers his or her credibility is also at stake. You don't have to build too much rapport with a solicitor at this stage; they will become more involved as the project gains momentum.

Let's go back to the reservoir of resources critical to your success. Understanding on which side of the spectrum you reside should help you identifying the gaps in your skill set. When you acknowledge your talents, and also areas you have not yet developed, you will have the ability to move forward. Don't fall into the trap of believing you can be all things to everyone; that is a slippery slope and you most likely will let everyone down and set yourself up for failure.

The next step in your evaluation process is to move your potential resources from "untrusted" to "lightly trusted." To put it simply, do not leap to fully trusting your resources in a single bound. Go through multiple layers before you can allocate a preferred level of trust; once that level (let's say 30 percent) has been reached, then it is up to the individual resources to earn as much of your trust as you allow them to. It's a step in the right direction for those resources, and they should appreciate it greatly.

A great place to start when determining whom to lightly trust is to talk to a business coach or life coach. A coach will add a tremendous amount of value to your constant growth as an entrepreneur. The ideal thing about coaches with a talent for keeping smart people grounded is that they won't be interested in your idea or how your revenue can benefit them. They will be focused solely on helping you and guiding you through your journey, encouraging you see beyond the next few years, and passing on skills and experiences to you on the way. If you live in the moment, there is more chance you will absorb what works for you. You will not be able to absorb all the advice you are given; it's up to you to take what you like, make it part of your business acumen or moral compass, and build on your capabilities. The business coach or life coach will tell you what they believe your weaknesses are and assess your confidence levels and overall determination.

More times than not, coaches will observe rather than act, at least in the beginning. They don't usually focus on specifics; instead, they use high-level tactics to motivate you toward completion. Expect them to tell you things you disagree with from time to time. Don't reject the process straight away, but think positively about the conversations and glean as much knowledge as you can. Even though you may not immediately agree about the principles under discussion, don't discard them. In fact, the discussions may highlight things to which you need to pay more attention. If you struggle with process and motivation, as many of us do, a business coach or life coach can help you move to the next level.

The next resource you should identify is a marketing company. There is no point engaging the company at this stage; just keep it on your radar until the right moment presents itself. If you maintain a constant speed and momentum, the time to engage the next resource will become clear. Continue checking potential resources from time to time to ensure they are reputable, profitable, and ethical. Individuals may lack ethics or compassion during certain periods of their lives; however, a company that is seeking to engage you as a new client will remain professionally supportive. We talk more about marketing and other resources in the coming chapters.

Always identify resources first without engaging them at any level. Be vague if you need to be, and don't demonstrate trust. Many great inventions have been undone and failed to reach the marketplace because their inventors trusted others to soon. Most people are computer literate these days and have adopted social media in an aggressive way. Remember that the Internet is a brutal playground. I mention this because one accidental Facebook or blog post, Tweet, or email can bring your idea to its knees much faster than you thought possible. We are innovators; we are not bulletproof.

When you select the group of individuals who will advise you, base your selections on their experience and alignment with your project outcomes. This group of individuals will generally fall into one of three categories—industry specific, business acumen, and finance/accountancy. Take the example of an application designed to run on a technical platform such as Android or iOS. Ensure that someone on your team has extensive knowledge of the application world or can add contacts to the ever-growing list of people whom you will lightly trust, without causing too much overlap.

Once you have a small group of industry-aware individuals, identify those who have run a business in the past or have been part of a growing and successful startup organization. These people may have held lengthy management positions or have business educational backgrounds related to your project. At some point in the future, you may consider hiring a part-time managing director, if you feel that role falls outside your skill set. The life of the business will always emanate from you, but always hold the company's best interests at heart.

# Move to Trusting Someone

The information in the previous chapters should have stimulated your mind enough to ensure your journal and documentation preparation is well underway. Perhaps, however, we can take the opportunity to make some adjustments.

Let's go over the group of resources again, and consider how we can build our confidence level to take the step toward trusting your key resources. You should have an accountant in mind, a business coach ready to go (if you haven't already engaged in an agreement with one), a technology partner in mind, and a marketing company ready and able to launch on cue. A key resource we haven't spoken a great deal about is your "sounding board." Discussing this resource can be as painful as pulling teeth for some entrepreneurs and often makes us shift nervously in our chairs. It is time to test the idea by delicately sharing your idea with a trusted resource, one who will remain outside your inner circle of work colleagues, but close enough to hold an open and honest conversation with you.

This person can be a family member or your business coach. My external trusted resources are my aunt and uncle, both intelligent people from different spectrums of the entrepreneurial scale, and more than capable of explaining their thoughts without sparking any emotional responses. Perfect. You are not giving away your intellectual property; just sharing high-level concepts and gaining feedback. They may see something you have missed something or have valid suggestions about your list of resources. The sounding board creates an interesting battleground, mostly because they won't understand your idea at first and may see holes in your strategy due to missing dots they are struggling to connect. They just don't get it. However, stick with these people and focus on getting your message across, which is sometimes easier said than done. If you cannot communicate your idea to your sounding board because there are no prototypes at this stage, you will have to develop a better communication method. That way, you won't leave investors or the buying community perplexed as you drive on by.

It's not all doom and gloom. I have done this many times, and I still feel frustrated if my sounding board doesn't understand me right away. I have since learned that it's okay, because they will have the same criticism as the consumer when you sell your new product or service to the public. Any structural feedback you can obtain most likely reflects the thought process of the consumer and may be something as simple as "you should use yellow, yeah, yellow is more attractive." I'm not suggesting you take all the feedback from your sounding board. Just be sure to select the person or people based on their honesty; a "yes" person is the worst possible choice.

A business or life coach is the next person you should begin to trust. It is a great way to grow your skills with anonymity. At the beginning, the coach will be focused on your personal growth and on helping you see things that you may otherwise miss on a day-to-day basis. He or she will focus on your operational methods, your interaction with others, and your current confidence levels, with a view toward increasing them over time. If this person helps you with daily motivation or strategy, keep going and move onto more detailed concerns, such as those you have about your weaknesses. If the coach connects well with you, and you feel as though you are getting along at a high level, then he or she will remain valuable to you.

We have previously highlighted the pungent negatives of the social media landscape. However, you will eventually need a functional website and online presence. Quick note: just because you're preparing to go online with your product does not mean you should confuse this with your personal life. Once you place your digital footprint onto any social medium, there is very little you can do to take it back. Please keep business separate from family, focus on product activities only, and don't cross-pollinate. If you are not an excellent web designer or graphic artist, there are plenty to choose from. Do your research, and avoid companies that charge too much ($5,000); instead look for those companies whose fees are more realistic ($1,000–$2,000). Chances are they will be just as good and will fight for your business above and beyond the top companies. You may even decide to develop the product design or website overseas such as Europe, AsiaPac, India or China; that can be cost-effective and produce excellent outcomes.

As you move to trusting your technical experts, avoid putting too much pressure on yourself to get the design right the first time. On average, companies alter their online design and marketing strategies every two years, and potentially rebrand every five. The only goal to focus on while trusting this group is to get something off the ground so you can start trading when the time is right. Having a website to showcase your product is a great motivator; look at it every day, if you feel like it, and deep dive to drive the project to conclusion. The IT environment is highly saturated, and companies will fight for your business. Enjoy the attention, and choose three companies to create competition when requesting a quote.

It's time to trust your selected marketing company to create awareness of how close your product is to completion and think about creative designs and marketing strategies. Don't hand over any money at this point; allow the company to show you a sample of its work that is similar to your product concept. Push back on any requested down payments or upfront charges. Let company representatives know that you have two other firms to choose from, and encourage them to put their best foot forward—from design to cost.

Once you select the right marketing company, staff there will have your best interests at heart, as long as you are a reliable client. Good and responsive marketing companies provide outstanding work, and will typically move as fast as you possible can, remember though, they will move on quickly at the conclusion of any project. Don't make them your new best friend, they are a resource on your Project conveyor belt.

Now you have a trusted group or resources waiting to begin the next step of your project. The reason I mentioned earlier about lightly trusted resources is because you should never give away your entire trust to any one person or any company, no matter how good they are. You have already allocated a percentage of trust to your resources, so begin to look at the collective resources as a whole. You are lightly trusting them already and are more than aware by now how you allocate trust. The best that an external resource can ever hope to achieve in the realm of trust is about 50 percent. Never give away all your trust, and always be vigilant toward your trusted resources. They may be great people, but they work for you. You are the client, the customer. Don't become buddy-buddy with them, because they will drop the ball and make you less of a priority. It may happen behind the scenes, but it will happen. The very second you communicate that your suppliers have gone above and beyond or done the best job ever, expect a few crappy months from the marketing folks.

Another piece of wisdom is to avoid going into business with family or friends. They will confuse your journey, and along the way your relationships may be damaged. You need to be able to hold your suppliers and resources accountable. It's difficult to achieve this outcome with family or friends with no love lost. Strong relationships are worth protecting, not tested.

# Expect Resistance

Resistance to change is engrained in the human DNA, I am absolutely convinced of that. We have evolved into a self-obsessed society that is more concerned about a smart device with a low battery charge than about missing a trip to the doctor. When a piece of plastic and glass has a global impact and the ability to generate a dramatic tipping point, it is sometimes hard to concentrate on the real world around you. A resistance mechanism used by modern, tech-savvy Internet social butterflies is to use a smart phone to compare an idea with what is already in the market. Such individuals may suggest that if you drop your price, they may purchase your product. Or provide feedback as to why they may be hesitant to buy, simply because the product is a different color than they expected.

For example, smart-phone-based, real-time research might occur during a romantic dinner at an expensive restaurant, where your companion is barely able to make eye contact or contribute to the conversation. This is because there are

Facebook updates to be entered, Tweets to send out, and Instagram photos of the meal to post online. Ah, true love warms the heart. This is a small example of what you can expect from the world of the consumer.

Allow me to focus on the three primary sources of resistance I encounter each time I dedicate effort to a new project. Typically, at inception, I barely understand the project, never mind family, friends, potential investors, and the broader consumer community. Resistance from family and friends most likely will come from a place of kindness. They want to protect you from yourself and are anxious that you are throwing away a wonderful career to which you have dedicated so much time, even if you work for McDonald's. Trust me when I say that because you are operating outside the box, they won't be able to contemplate that you are doing what you are most passionate about.

If your family are honest hard workers, they will see reason in the journey of the innovator and will push past their fear of danger and potential high risk. More often than not, they will sit down and have that all-inspiring heart-to-heart with you. They may explain that they care about you so much and don't want to see you fail. This conversation will happen if you're fourteen or forty. It's interesting to see how family and friends can be influenced by fear and make you nervous about your future. Simply reassure them that you are fine and on a smooth path to completing something you've always wanted to achieve. Advise them not to be so nervous. If feasible, tell them that you will still be working elsewhere to generate income.

Demonstrate to them that the project will not be put you in jeopardy, and ask them to think about the possibilities of success and the many opportunities that could come your way. You can see pretty clearly that this type of resistance comes from a good place. Unfortunately, resistance won't act as a motivator until later in the project, i.e., when family and friends start to come around to your way of thinking. Who knows, one day you might invest in or mentor another person's first journey into the world of the entrepreneur. By the time you have completed a few projects, you can quite easily become a lightly trusted resource for others.

Entrepreneurs often have high levels of common sense and energy levels, although it may not seem that way at the beginning. Many of us focus on the new idea and are completely dedicated to seeing it come to fruition, but we store some funds away for a rainy day or if the project runs longer than anticipated. As we work on our first invention or product, we often have full-time employment, and innovate on the side. While dedicating your excited time to the project, also focus on the need for savings or earning a supplementary income.

There are, of course, individuals who break this simple rule; they focus on their projects 100 percent and don't worry about maintaining a healthy bank balance. I don't believe your first project should be held to that level of risk, and it is my view that alternate sources of revenue are critical to the success of your project. If the people who throw around risk are successful, they may tell the story of how they invested their very last dime and lived like recluses, eating baked beans in order to see the project through to completion. These rags-to-riches stories are few and far between and seldom told with complete accuracy. I won't take anything away from "last dime" innovators. However, if you drill down you may find that although they did use their last dimes, they also had wealthy parents. People in general, though—entrepreneurs or otherwise—are motivated by these stories, because they spread hope that anyone can achieve his or her goals and dreams, overcome adversity, and perhaps change the world with one smart idea.

Once your documentation is up-to-date, and you have surrounded yourself with your trusted consortium while having completed a prototype or design details sufficient to demonstrate, it might be time to include an external investor in your group. Investors can act as fantastic motivators for your project and help you achieve your end goal—i.e., a market-ready product—far quicker than otherwise might be the case. They will come, however, with their own brand of resistance, one that is vastly different from that of family and friends. An investor's goal is simple: contribute as little financially as possible, gain as much owner's equity as possible, and ensure the return on investment is tangible and warrants the engagement from the beginning.

The good news is that there are numerous investors out there prepared to invest in promising new products, especially if the invention has potential to disrupt the marketplace. You will hit resistance until the investment deal is signed. Investors will push for a better financial outcome for themselves and even feign disinterest in your invention to drive down perceived value. More times than not, they will decide to contribute to the project after a few tedious rounds of legal paperwork. After an agreement has been struck, they will transition quickly from a negotiating entity to a support agent and contribute to the project with their own sets of skills to protect their investment. Investors might fill gaps in financial management or offer connections to a broader range of influential executives.

If the new business does not have a sellable product or revenue-driving brand yet, then you will need to sell the idea passionately and communicate a cost analysis for getting the project off the ground, with some conservative projections. Do not present your product to an investor with projected revenue of $4 billion; you won't achieve anything except more resistance. If you have taken your product to market and have some sales revenue, share that information with the investor to build confidence, including a breakdown of what it cost you to push your product to where it is today. A new idea that is limping in its infancy is more attractive to investors than a non-tangible thought. Mostly they are disinterested in high-earning products and equally disinterested if the idea is in the early stages of conception. They don't want to fund your time and effort to build it. Any financial injection must be directed toward product promotion that has a solid strategy and includes that all-important return on investment, not just a return for others, but for you as well.

You may trust your investors in the future, but please do not hand over trust just because money has exchanged hands. They are still an unproven entity. I heard the following analogy many years ago: "An investor is like a hitchhiker, everything will be smooth sailing if you are taking them in the direction they want to go. The second you deviate from that course they will knock you over the head and steal your wallet." They are not trusted resources until they prove themselves.

Okay, so now we have experienced resistance from family and friends and have taken the time to reassure them all is well and that you are not throwing your life away. You have also navigated the treacherous waters of finding an investor and have struck a palatable deal that makes everyone happy. Well, for the most part–you will never be 100 percent happy with your negotiations with an investor; accept a reasonable outcome and move forward. If you do not find an investor, don't panic; you'll be able to look for one again later in the process. If you need someone to check documents before you sign them, contact your solicitor or accountant.

A final source of resistance is the ever-present and sometimes fickle consumer. Whether your product has achieved mainstream awareness or is a specialty item sold via retail or distribution, the consumer will be your most honest and brutal critic. Consumers are more likely to discuss negative experiences within their sphere of influence; only a small percentage will share a positive experience. This is how consumers operate when in purchasing mode; they are always after a bargain and enjoy new products. One of the great contributions you can make to the consumer landscape is a unique product that addresses a broad problem or fills a need. If you have discovered a gap in the market and promote the *need* for your product above and beyond the *desire* for the product, you will be well positioned for a successful product launch and greater financial gain.

Typical resistance comments you may encounter from the consumer include:

- It's too expensive.
- Perhaps if there were a two-for-one deal.
- I think I can get it elsewhere for less.
- If only it were on sale.

Be reassured that this type of resistance has absolutely nothing to do with your product. Unfortunately, society has a lot to answer for when it comes to price modeling. Retail stores offer sales and discounts for members so frequently throughout the year, they dilute the value of any new product. Soon retailers find out the hard way that when they return their products to the recommended retail price (RRP), sales drop. It's an unsustainable model that has been adopted globally. Of course, some retailers deliberately set their prices higher than normal for a week or so, making a 50-percent discount appear way too attractive to pass up. I suggest you stay away from this model. Set your RRP, and try to stick to it for the long run. If you need motivation, then study the Apple pricing and partnership model. Apple never runs huge sales, and it never shifts from its RRP. But it provides excellent customer service for all of its innovative products.

How do we combat this relentless wave of consumer resistance? First, involve your marketing company prior to launching your product. It's the marketing company's job to build suspense around the product and to establish a marketing campaign for different demographics. You may advertise in America in a vastly differently way than you do so in Australia. A strategy that has worked for me in the past is to send out marketing materials and media releases a few weeks before the product is available. With clever marketing, you can create a level of suspense and curiosity that will generate interest. For example, you might advertise pre-orders prior to the launch; then you can offer something like a T-shirt to the first hundred people who commit to purchasing. But do not drop your RRP; there is no way to come back from lowering your price from the beginning for any reason.

The only time pricing becomes a negotiating point is when you are dealing with retailers or distributors prepared to stock your product. These organizations will want to meet your

RRP, but they won't want to pay your RRP. Typically, they will ask for about 50 percent or higher off RRP, in order to create a reasonable profit for themselves. A strong buying signal that you should leverage is when a retailer or distributor attempts negotiating exclusivity rights. You need leverage to create competition amongst the retailers etc. to drive the best financial outcome for your business.

Retailers can also provide you a terrible version of resistance, if they feel cheated on the price and don't feel that they have the upper hand. They may use their financial muscle to disrupt the success of your product. Watch out if they drop the price on similar products to keep you out of the market, or use negative marketing against you. Don't panic; the larger retailers operate at a glacial pace, and you will have time on your side. The key is to strike a happy balance with the retailer, so that the way forward will be clear for both sides. In addition, they may insist that you can no longer sell you're your product while they are stocking it, you may become your own competitor. These are not negative outcomes, if the retailer begins managing and holding stock for you it removes the need for you to manage end to end logistics. Also, having your product on the shelves of major retailers is strong marketing in itself and a great way to breakdown resistance from consumers.

Your marketing company will be well aware of consumer resistance and should be able to compile a reasonable strategy to attract your target market directly or via a suitable retailer. It's important to understand that the land of the consumer is an entity unto its own, they are always aware, so don't use a technology retailer to stock you new swimwear line. Not many people understand the consumer mindset in a way that can trigger buying habits, certainly not across multiple demographics. Never be disappointed. Be prepared, and expect that your product may not appeal to everyone or may face a significant amount of resistance.

As mentioned above, if your product fits a need and not a want, your sales potential will rise exponentially. If it is unique to the marketplace, hold on tight, because that differentiates a fantastic product. Ensure your patents are in order; ask your solicitor to help. If the product is marketed vibrantly, using buying triggers other than mainstream products, you should be okay. When marketing, demonstrate the illuminating factors about your product that make it differ from anything else available. With any luck, your invention will be unique and will capture a corner of the market before anyone else tries to replicate it. Don't be afraid if someone does so; you will always be able to advertise your product as the original, which does carry weight with the consumer.

A few minor strategies before we leave resistance from the consumer. Use any positive feedback you receive straight away to highlight your product's quality. When you receive positive feedback, place it on the packaging, on your website, and even on all your business social media forums. Positive feedback is a slice of gold if the reference comes from an educated person in your selling vertical. For example, if you release a medical device, a reference or comment from the lead professor at a reasonably sized hospital will slingshot your product into the realm of notoriety and profitability.

Now that we have discussed my top resistance points, let's examine the possibility that groups of resistance will all come at once or will overlap. If you find yourself trying to appease your family while negotiating with an investor and addressing a consumer concern, remain calm. This can be a highly stressful situation, but you can manage by taking the time to think. Remember to keep your head and remain focused on the success of your product. Prioritize which resistance group to address first and methodically work through the situation. If necessary, reread the first chapter, "Don't Be Afraid"; then focus on the long-term goal. Change your mindset and refocus; you will easily see things for what they are—simple obstacles.

If your family care about you and are not consumed by stress themselves, they will wait for you to explain your journey. If your investors sees true value in your product and show you a buying signal by indicating their willingness to wait, then you are in good stead. If consumers are a stressful point of resistance, try passing them off to one of your trusted resources; perhaps marketing can send out a press release to appease to masses. Or ask your trusted consortium to help you manage the workload. That's why you spent so much time establishing the group—so you wouldn't always have to do the heavy lifting. Before you know it, this period will subside, and you'll be back promoting your product and planning to build revenue. Take a deep breath and keep going; never stand still.

If you get the product part right, you will have something tangible to show your family, a history of revenue to show the investor, and a positive financial track record to market to the consumer. You will have turned a difficult situation into a win. Many of the parties who once provided resistance now will have what they need to believe in you and your product.

I will leave this chapter with a few references from Thomas Edison, an inspiration to me and an inventor who faced incredible resistance.

- "I have not failed, I've just found 10,000 ways that won't work."
- "I never did a day's work in my life, it was all fun."
- "If we did all the things we are capable of, we would literally astound ourselves."

# Mind Games

Humans have a built-in mechanism of survival, an internal desire to live that is so strong, we generally proceed in ignorance. This inbuilt characteristic worked for cavemen, who had a heightened level of adrenaline, which governs the fight-or-flight response. Their greatest motivation was to avoid dangerous predators, unless they are the ones being hunted for food. Among modern day men and women, that same survival instinct still exists; however, we dedicate a good portion of it to viewing others as potential threats. Over time, we create huge battlegrounds, where mind games thrive. Everyone plays them to varying degrees—from innocent white lies to exaggerations to corporate assassination and bullying. People will attempt to manipulate you for fun or control of your assets, and you may not even realize others are playing mind games. Both awareness of participating in mind games, and partial or complete ignorance are equally scary scenarios. Realize that life isn't fair; it never has been, and chances are it never will be.

Refer to the chapters "Don't Be Afraid" and "Beware the Narcissist" to determine what to look out for. If you've followed the trust model described in this book, you will combat the mind games directed at you without applying dedicated thought to the process. Trusting no one will prevent anyone from getting close enough; however, this may also motivate others to try harder to get to you. You must remain vigilant. If they do get their way and cause damage to your brand or make you shift your focus, you will become incredibly distraught. However, they will sleep soundly at night. Use the defensive mechanisms described in the "Trust No One" chapter to deflect attempts from others who try to infiltrate your thinking space.

The individuals who are adept at mind games sometimes have nothing to gain. Playing games has fed their egos for so long it has evolved into a sport. Knowing this to be true, let's discuss some common mind games that may be played within your operating space. For the purpose of giving titles to the negative people we encounter, I will refer to them as either narcissists or intruders.

Small mind games won't influence you if you don't allow them to; assigning trust is always within your control. An analogy I often use in presentations is the comparison between narcissistic mind games and Internet trolls, who can be relentless. Unfortunately, they are winning the battle against normality. I don't even pretend to see what is happening inside the mind of an Internet troll. Those who are Internet savvy may have come across them in the past; they are lost individuals whose sole purpose is to boost their own self-confidence by unnecessarily attacking others. Basically, they are online digital bullies.

Like all bullies, they don't enjoy being ignored and may step up their mind games. That is one main reason I suggested you have a digital presence only for your product, and post nothing personal online. Most honest people are not equipped to deal with Internet trolls. Don't panic; there are methods you can employ to remain distant from the Internet vermons. I suggest you ignore them all the time and certainly do not respond to them emotionally, no matter what they have said. In fact, don't respond at all; it's just not worth it. Once you are highly successful you may learn about better ways to manage trolls. For example, singer James Blunt was being unnecessarily attacked for the brilliance of his music, bombarded with comments such as "you have no talent," "you have no skills," "you have nothing at all." Blunt responded, "Or a mortgage."

The strategic mind game is another very common event that occurs a little closer to home or perhaps in your workplace. These are the situations in which strangers attempt to befriend you and get all buddy-buddy with you, motivated by their own needs and wants. They will use their well-rehearsed powers of influence to slowly infiltrate your personal space. These mind games are dangerous because the intruders are prepared to wait. They have patience, and they are willing to dedicate what it takes to become a trusted resource to get closer to understanding your potential.

A red flag identifying this type of intruder may take place during the initial encounter when you display confidence and excitement in your ideas. These trust chasers will employ everything in their mind-game reservoirs to win you over. Their goal is simple: to identify your potential and work out how they can benefit from it. If you have not adhered to the skills discussed in "Trust No One," which shows you how to create a solid defense mechanism, they will eventually convince you they are genuine and get close enough to influence your success. They will praise you as a person and your clever way of thinking; what they are actually thinking is, "how can I get a cut of this success, and bring more money my way?" This is called fraudulently taking a cut of the winnings. You don't usually make friends this fast; don't start now.

As I've said before, don't panic. I have a strategy that should hold you in good stead. Let's assume the worst for a second. Imagine that someone has managed to get through your defense mechanisms and now is one of your trusted resources. Your obliviousness to this is most likely is due to the fact you are on the inside of your project, operating under the hood, and may not have a high-level, holistic view of the situation.

The intruders may become so close to you that your emotional side may allow them to remain involved. That is a mistake. It may be difficult for you to disengage from intruders if you allow them to become too engrained in your creative process. They may even convince you that without them your project won't reach its full potential, that you might have a larger impact on the marketplace if they are cut in on the deal, and that failure is in the cards unless they are involved. This type of thinking has a way of snowballing out of control, and you may not realize the full toxicity of the situation until it's fully embedded. I have a cute analogy to describe this problem and a great solution.

Remember your first romantic partner in high school or university? Perhaps you found yourself in a situation that was a little destructive. It was your first venture into the world of romance, but you found out over time that it was no longer something with which you wanted to be involved. However, you could not bring yourself to break up because you didn't want to upset your partner. You put your wishes second to keep the status quo. You may even be the type of person who is happy to remain unhappy in order to keep the peace; it's a common entrepreneurial trait. It would have been heartbreaking to break up, and because you're human, you will feel a little drained by the emotional experience.

Perhaps you backed away from conflict and had one of your friends break up for you. (Remember, you were young with little world experience.) Once done, the pain subsides over time, and ultimately you convinced yourself you made the right decision. Perhaps you now have the strength to initiate breakups yourself, because as you grow older and wiser you see things a little differently. But back then, the job was done, however painful it might have been. I affectionately refer to the person who broke up with your partner on your behalf as the "bulldog"—highly valuable and highly protective of you.

When an intruder infiltrates your circle of influence and drives your idea in a different direction than its original trajectory, you will find yourself in a very awkward position. Either you will see that this person has been playing mind games to get close to you for their own benefit, or a friend or colleague will tell you that this person does not care about you, your ideas, and are only looking to benefit financially from your success. Waking up to this realization may make you nervous, but it is a positive event. Awareness that you need to address this issue is a critical and motivating step forward. And now you know how to get the intruder out of your life: you bring in your bulldog.

The bulldog will be someone you trust, someone who has no emotional attachment to your ideas or projects. He or she is simply there to support you when you need it and will be mildly frustrated when someone else tries to exploit you. The bulldog ultimately is the best person to help you remove the intruder from your life before things get worse. Don't be afraid; this could be fun, especially when you are proven correct. After all, the intruder has been playing you long enough; it's time for a little payback. Long story short, when you engage your bulldog, he or she will have no hesitation about breaking the news that you no long want to be affiliated with the intruder, whose financial requests are for amounts that are far greater than they deserve and will dilute the value of your project commitments. By the way, it's not cowardly to allow others to fill a role that you struggle over because you are focused on your project. You're on a journey of success; jump over roadblocks using whatever method you find most palatable. A final point on this particular topic: Once the bulldog has dealt with the intruders and they have moved to a distance, intruders will contact you directly and use their most convoluted mind games to keep you on board. Ignore their emotional appeals, and simply say, "It's best if we are not part of the same venture," and move on. Hang up the phone, close the chat, or end the instant messenger session—whatever it takes. They won't be back any time soon. Love the bulldog.

Let's discuss the open forum mind game. This is where intruders make it so obvious that they want to support you, no one believes they are playing mind games. These types of intruder use their size to become intimidating. They are often tall and have a dominating presence. People who are not involved in the mind games often see what is happening but are not courageous enough to intervene. Intruders generally have narcissistic tendencies, but perhaps they are not full-blown narcissists. They are often passive-aggressive and confidently drift through life, convinced that they are better than those around them. They differ from true narcissists, because they genuinely believe what they say and believe is true. True narcissists destroy your relationships and leave a trail of carnage in their wake.

Intruders would never consider their tactics to be intense mind games. They focus on reducing the confidence of others, dismantling relationships, and feeding their constantly hungry egos. One day, you will see how confused they become when others stop hanging on their every word. When they fail, their true colors will briefly come out for all to see. It's interesting to watch, but remain a distant and vigilant observer. Do not become involved in the motives of this mind game expert.

I label this style of mind game as an open forum arena, because intruders do not care what others think about them. They will bounce back from any loss of confidence. They believe that making public statements in an open forum gives everyone the false illusion that they are genuine and probably experienced a bad couple of days. They think about their heightened advantage and gaming capabilities; as they play their mind games in the open forum it becomes easier to identify their next target. The new focal person will appear easy to influence, in need of something the intruders can provide, and a little desperate for acceptance and gratification.

Above, I described the top three mind games being played today. Of course, the games will differ depending on personalities; however, they are fairly consistent in the way they evolve. Chances are you will not be ready to retaliate, and to be honest, that isn't the goal anyway. Instead, focus on being resilient. Refer to previous chapters in this book and entries in your journal to help you become more conscious of the mind games that surround you.

Here are a couple of early detection mechanisms. (I know it sounds dramatic, but if you don't let these people into your life they cannot disrupt your journey.) If you are at a social function, work or otherwise, take a moment to survey the room and observe anyone whom you believe is acting disingenuous. These people often move quickly from group to group, introducing themselves as key resources and under high demand for their talents. I recommend you focus on two things that are understated and not taught well, but are by far the greatest tools you have above and beyond words: body language and eye contact.

Observe the body language of intruders. You will see them move into people's personal space. They may talk while they look around the room. They shake hands confidently with the group, using their girth as leverage, and hand out business cards. Once they feel confident, they will move on to another group and repeat this pattern until they have spoken to everyone in the room.

Pay close attention to the body language of the people who engage with an intruder. Are they slouching, paying strong attention, or shuffling nervously because they are not sure what to take away from this encounter? Take note of when eye contact fails. If the people in the room remain personable with good eye contact, yet the intruder avoids eye contact and already seems interested in the next group, don't engage them. These people often want to know sooner rather than later "Are you with me or against me?" They are playing games and won't be interested in anything other than extracting your ideas and being a part of your project for their own financial gain. It's sometimes difficult to remain focused, but body language and eye contact really do sum up a person. Learn to pay close attention to the basics, and you will avoid confrontations and reduce risk in the future.

Finally, the most dangerous intruder is the person who is adept at manipulating and influencing people, and, for whatever reason, have nothing to lose. Perhaps they are having difficulties at home, missed out on that promotion, or have actually hit rock bottom. No matter whom you cross paths with, never assume you know enough about them to judge. Distractions can also occur if individuals are too involved in playing mind games and do not focus enough on their own lives. Playing games is no longer a challenge; it is a necessity that keeps them sane.

I have encountered these intruders in the past and found it difficult, because they are backed into a corner with nothing to lose—the most dangerous motivator of all time. These intruders often need an escape and only find relief when they project their fear and anxiety onto others. The trouble always starts with empathetic people who consider it their personal responsibility to help someone in need. They see the pain and want to bring this person to a happier state of mind. Do not be that person! As sad as it is, we must be wary of empathy; it will leave you vulnerable, and give intruders a new target to make them feel a little bit better.

It's great to be a nice person, but ask yourself if you have helped too many people when they are in trouble, especially those you haven't known long. You may be a sensitive person and a caring person, and no one can take that away from you. Just be diligent about with whom and how you choose to empathize with. Know your boundaries; you cannot be all things to everyone. There are plenty of professionals out there to help others; it's not your responsibility to try and fix people, inherently people cannot be fixed, they need to do that themselves in conjunction with proper help. I have seen it too many times, and the fallout is often devastating.

# Beware of the Narcissist

Your entrepreneur fund reservoir is an imaginary vault that holds anything unique to you or that you want kept to yourself. This includes everything from personal financial wealth, knowledge, and experience all the way to contacts in your selected industry. These are the "funds" you will use to build your idea and complete your project.

This chapter may make you feel uneasy and a little nervous, although that is not my intent. Narcissists have the potential to destroy businesses, relationships, and practically anything in the way of what they want. Remember that the true devastation of what they can achieve sometimes rises at an exponential rate and might pose a very real threat to you and your project. As such, it's smart to identify the tools narcissists have at their disposal, so we can manage the positive outcome we want for ourselves and our projects without their influence. Let's first discuss some of things to look out for and then examine tools that we can add to our arsenals.

By the way, there is nothing wrong with the simple word "hello." That's all you need to say when talking to a narcissist. You are not out to make a new best friend to motivate you and share in your success. You are seeking responsible people with genuine intent to grow positively when they are around you. A narcissist may fall into one of three categories:

- Someone you just met out of the blue
- Someone you met before you had your new idea
- A family member.

Yes, as sad as it sounds many narcissists are related to entrepreneurs and have always harbored a deep jealously for what they have or are capable of achieving.

A narcissist hides behind the façade of a normal individual, one who is often polite and conscientious. Never judge a book by its cover. It can take some time to learn how to identify a narcissist; however, once you recognize the red flags you will quickly understand the best way to react and how to end the relationship quickly. Narcissists hide their true persona due to their unhappiness within themselves, built-up hatred for others succeeding around them, internal anger, concealed bitterness, and the belief that the world owes them something. They are often happy to project these internal stressors onto you and anyone who will listen during their journey of destruction. The world doesn't actually owe them anything, and our willingness to make our own way in the world escapes them. Some narcissists expect to be able to take something from another person simply because they want it more. They will use many tactics to achieve that goal, often by approaching those around you.

When people offer gifts to your family members or friends, that should be an immediate red flag. Ask yourself why someone you hardly know is giving gifts, even though on the surface the generosity seems genuine. Gifts and financial support are tools they use to gain leverage over you. This will start to become clearer when you identify them as narcissists. Another bright red flag is when they "casually" mention these gifts. For example: "Remember when I paid for us to go to that conference. That was fun, right?" Or "Did your niece end up using that iPad I gave her? I hope it helped." And even less subtly: "You should wear that shirt I bought you more often; it looks good on you." The age-old rule applies, no matter how old you are: don't borrow from friends or family, and don't accept gifts or candy from strangers!

Narcissists will spend time to see if they can extract money from you or benefit from your idea succeeding. They often wait very patiently as they are planning. They have a few goals and many, already-established tools, developed during a long career in the destruction of relationships. I believe destruction is built into their DNA. They will try and drag you down subtly behind your back and will often manipulate stories to cement their foothold over you, slowly gaining power and influence over you and your project. In reality they are planting the seed of doubt in you and those you engage with, and will nurture the seed just long enough to disrupt your project.

If their plans to disrupt your project do not work out, narcissists eventually will try and drag you down directly to your face. This is a dangerous stage because of the intense nature of the confrontation that may occur. Be under no illusion; the beasts who are narcissists will either explode, dragging you down with them, or feed their own internal self-doubt and plan to strike again. It is a great outcome is if they just exit your life with a harsh character attack; at least, they are gone.

One thing is certain: they want to project their own fear and anxiety onto you as a way to gain control. In addition, they will be very frustrated and angry if they fail. Once a narcissist told me in a fit of anger, "If you worked for me I would fire you" How amusing. He had finally realized that he would never gain access to my funds; he openly threw a tantrum and stormed off. While this was a great outcome for me—as it removed one of the losers from my life in an open corporate environment—jealousy and bitterness runs deeply within these people and only festers over time. If they have tried once already, they may see a second or third attempt as a challenge. They are relentless!

Let's now discuss the fundamental tools you have at your disposal for identifying narcissists, react swiftly, and calmly getting them out of your life. Pay attention to the signals. Narcissists are people who comment that they are always right, and fabricate back stories to build a rapport with you. In reality they only want access to your funds and will most likely be unhappy and frustrated with their own lives, no matter the outcome. Narcissists are extremely toxic to you and society as a whole. Look out for lonely, empty executives who don't appear ever capable of being whole.

It's critically important to understand the motivation of the narcissist. Once we understand the beast, we can fight the fight worth fighting, which is the survival of your project. Narcissists are excellent at concealing their strong sense of jealousy, deep-seated bitterness, vengeful sadistic sides, and most important, their desire to be at the top, no matter how many people they step on along the way. Often they are the ones who are asked how they sleep at night or how they live with themselves. Beware of their answers, because it's probably as disturbing as "well, I sleep on a pile of money, and I love myself because I am never wrong."

Again, it may sound dramatic but you must remove the losers from your life. One method is a simple tool called the ladder of influence. Take a pen and paper, and draw a ladder; place yourself and your family on the top rung and everyone else on the rungs below, in order of reliability and connection to you. For example, the second rung might contain extended family, while the third rung is high school friends with whom you are still in touch. As you work your way down your ladder, you will find that people in your circle of acquaintances probably don't need to be there or have drawn on your knowledge fund, distracting you from your goal—i.e., to finish your project.

Simply and kindly slow down your interactions with these people, and keep conversations with them very clinical. Pay particular attention to their attempts to make a withdrawal from your fund reservoir. The top rung of the ladder holds by far your most important priority.

One of the major ways to identify narcissists is to see how they react to being left out of the loop. They may seem a little put off if you explain your ideas to someone else, especially if you don't consulting them first. It's incredibly frustrating for narcissists when they are not in control of someone else. They build resentment that is so well hidden, you may never actually become aware of it. The worst thing that can happen is if they enter your community under the guise of moral support. They may invite themselves to meetings and other events, all the while chipping away at your defense layers and building rapport with your connections. It is critical that they have the acceptance of your peers; it's their best tool for bringing you down and creating corporate doubt in your abilities.

Be mindful of your surroundings and those you speak to; that will enable you to successfully read and decipher body language. Narcissists often have a telltale sign that they are frustrated with the current conversation; they may cross their arms or say something like "right, let's start again." Often they will try to repeat the conversation to sway the outcome their way and somehow convince you of their importance. If they fail, they may seem to accept the outcome for now, but they will try again later.

Another warning sign is to gauge how close a person stands near you. Ask yourself if there is any need for anyone to stand so close to you, and don't be afraid to step back to create space in your comfort zone. This is not a sign of weakness, but the establishment of boundaries. Some narcissists will be taller or louder than you are; this is an unfortunate gift for them, which creates an impression of dominance. Don't pay any attention. You can establish a level playing field by suggesting that you both take a seat or setting up a roundtable discussion to take place later in the comfort of your office environment. If you still doubt whether you see narcissistic tendencies in people, make sure you constantly stand your ground. The sign to watch for is their insistence on having discussions when and how they want to. They will pressure you to make a decision even when you are not ready and aim to take over the direction and finances of the project. Don't entertain this as an option.

Puppeteering is a common narcissist tool, often used to manipulate others to help extract information from you. They may be cunning and meet in private with your acquaintances and advisors, thinking that if they win them over, getting to you will be that little bit easier. It is concerning if you catch them doing this, as they are taking an "outside in" approach to get to you. If caught, they often plead innocence, and try and convince you that they were working in your best interests. This will make you weary and, again, should encourage you to get the loser out of your life.

Don't worry about turning your back on these people, they are more than happy to stab you in the chest. As discussed earlier, if things don't go their way, they won't be easily stopped. The trick is to recognize who they are as fast as possible and react accordingly to prevent any situation from festering out of control. A good tactic is to always have a third person present during your discussions with a "maybe narcissist"; this person may be a long-term business partner, friend in the same industry, or even a secretary, who can take notes. The more the individual pushes back on having anyone else around during meetings, the more you should aim to move him or her from a "maybe narcissist" to a "narcissist."

Being an entrepreneur includes many things that present a highly entertaining experience and a scary journey all at the same time. You are in control of the output you give to others; it's perfectly fine to say a simple "hello," and walk on by.

# Business Tools

Mastering business tools will be your key to the success of the project. Most entrepreneurs don't kick off their first projects with clear plans for developing budgets, maintaining health, and acquiring key resources. We need to make sure we use the tools wisely in order to increase our ability to succeed. It is the nature of the entrepreneur to approach anything creative in a chaotic way; it can take a fair amount of discipline to stick to plans and use resources wisely.

Business tools are not always physical or tangible. It is *not* about the things you don't have and more about using the things you do have efficiently and effectively. Learning to leverage your tools is the best way to learn how to approach your goals. A healthy body and mind, along with your charisma and your passion, may be your most valuable assets; it does depend on what you are trying achieve. It's critical to have a strong awareness of the industry you want to infiltrate and a thorough understanding of your competitors, if any. If you don't know how your business vertical is changing, you may find yourself quickly slipping behind. When you future-proof your idea, you may have to adjust it slightly to ensure that—by the time the project is completed—the market still sees your idea as highly desirable. Let's look at some valuable business tools you can use to increase the potential success of your project.

A timeframe is a good place to start; remember, not to work in absolutes. Giving yourself six months to complete your project and then struggling to deliver on time is an example of being too rigid upfront. Keep a realistic timeframe and give yourself plenty of time to nurture the idea. I like to start with a two-year timeframe, keeping in mind that sometimes it is smart to "fail fast" and move on. A good timeline shows you how to articulate your idea and share your project views in a way that can be constructively examined and discussed.

Consider using a calendar to create a timeline that tracks the beginning of your project through to completion with times and dates of meetings, events along the way, dedicated effort to the project, and time spent planning and working with your trusted resource group. If your calendar is online or stored on your computer, back it up regularly. I will discuss the importance of this shortly.

List daily tasks to help keep you on track. A directionless mindset will affect the project schedule, particularly if the entrepreneur develops any type of mental block. A task list will inspire you to think about the next task. Use the list as a motivator, because there is value in projecting forward; the end goal becomes clearer and remains exciting.

Another business tool, one referenced in earlier chapters, is your journal. Keep this collection of thoughts and vision for the product you are inventing or improving in an easily accessible place. For example, an online application that is compatible with your smart phone will allow you to update the journal on the go. Or use the text-editing program on your computer. From legal point of view, if you document your idea in your journal, you have evidence that it has been your idea from the beginning. Although you have trusted resources, many people will try to steal your ideas and capitalize on your future success. As mentioned earlier, trust is your possession and should be given only lightly.

These business tools—your calendar, task lists, and journal—can serve as proof of your invention and ideas built around it. Here is another little slice of gold: a tactic I have learned over time suggested by my patent solicitor, is to make copies of these three items. Photocopies or scanned documents are fine. Sign and date the originals; add a photo of yourself, also signed on the back. Then mail them to yourself, using guaranteed delivery and the sign-on-arrival option. When the package arrives a couple of days later, don't open it; simply file it away somewhere safe. If someone challenges your invention in a court of law, you will be able to produce a dated package that contains all your information. This will stand up in court, if necessary. Hopefully, you won't ever have to go through any legal proceedings; however it's best to be prepared and two steps ahead of copy cats. Documentation is important.

Let's look at some digital business tools, such as a budgeting program. It's very easy to lose track of expenditures; however, you'll need to track your spending for taxation and business purposes. Your budget should include your cost of goods, sales potential, cost of resources, how much you have spent, and how much you still plan to spend. Consider development costs; if your product will be built in a foreign country, there will be manufacturing and transport costs, including import and customs fees. You may need a storage facility to hold stock, depending on the volume of your first delivery. This is a little easier if you have negotiated a comprehensive agreement with a retailer, which will have its own well-organized logistics and distribution centers with plenty of warehouse space. Of course if your idea is digital or intangible, these concerns will not apply.

Depending on your personality, and on which side of the entrepreneurial spectrum you place yourself, you may choose to hire an external negotiator to manage your deals and opportunities. It's always a smart move to bring into your business people who can cover large gaps in your skills. We have discussed this a few times now; everyone has gaps in his or her abilities. Your task is to identify your gaps and find a resource that can fill them. An external negotiator is similar to your bulldog; you will pay this person to represent you in the best possible light and to obtain the greatest outcome. Do not be misled; you will find yourself in a negotiating position more times than not, with or without the negotiator. Be wary of the people across the table who say, "It's okay, we're not negotiating," because there is a high chance that they are.

 Never talk to someone about your business or sales model, especially when dealing with corporate or high-end retailers. They will manipulate your words and are more likely better at negotiating than you are. Don't panic, though; the contract negotiator comes in handy, and adds great value—driving you toward more revenue, higher sales, and greater exposure. A negotiation often will have a great track record in negotiating with retailers, from pricing models to mergers and acquisitions.

Your negotiator will become one of your trusted resources, but remember that he or she is paid to work in your best interests. The negotiator will work with your other trusted resources to identify your true cost analysis, sales and market potential, and revenue targets. Once you complete a true analysis of your production costs, you can work on the pricing model for your new business. How much does it cost to build and deliver the product? What margin you expect to add to the product price to bring it up to your projected RRP? By how much are you willing to reduce the RRP to honor your distribution agreement with a retailer that wants to purchase the product at cost. Stand your ground and create competition with other retailers to ensure the best outcome for you and your business.

The contract negotiator is an invaluable business tool for jumping over hurdles in any business transaction.

Our next business tool is the ever-present and very dangerous realm of the Internet. It's important to build skills in online navigating to help you acquire knowledge, enhance your marketing efforts and resources, and keep a close eye on potential competitors and copycats. There are companies whose sole purpose is to conduct online searches for new products and determine if the inventors have protected their intellectual property rights. These companies circumvent the rules by slightly adjusting products that are performing well in the marketplace and developing their own brands. You too should be resourceful about finding information and building knowledge. Although it is not broadly advertised, teams of people around the globe are attempting to infiltrate businesses of all types. Corporate espionage is alive and well.

We now live in a world in which we are always connected—at least, via the Internet—to just about everything else. Being online will always pose a medium to high risk, and that risk will grow exponentially. In short, the Internet is an active project focused on by corporations and essentially aims to be the foundation to achieve large steps involving emerging technology. The goal is to establish communication between anything that can connect to the Internet, and evolve the things that are currently disconnected. Things that have already become connected to the Internet via the "Internet of Things" (IoT) include fridges, TVs, home-based electronics, as well as cars and buses, medical equipment, plains, boats, homes and people. New things on the technology roadmap range from wallets and purses to human mobility implants and health monitors implanted in skin tissue. Cashless supermarkets and digital stores are already a reality; however, they will need to increase their footprint over time, and the financial economy we know today will change. Imagine using a taxi, bus, train, or airplane without having to do anything other than get on board. Think about your bank accessing an electronic chip implanted within you to complete and verify your payments. Medical monitors will track your vitals and determine if it is safe for you to fly; other devices may take blood samples on the go, in the event of a medical emergencies. It is interesting and exciting to see today's technology era unfold before our eyes. However, nothing is sacred or safe on the Internet. In a connected world, information is readily available to anyone who looks for it and cannot be easily removed from such an active and deeply imbedded Public medium.

When it comes to your business, ask your IT resources to help you find information from different sectors of the Internet. A couple of my products are manufactured in China, so I researched Chinese manufacturers to see if anything similar had been produced there. It is very easy to do, and given the ease of engagement and difficulty in production, you will find what you need. As discussed prior, the Internet is full of predators and false information. Always be diligent about protecting your ideas and innovations. Searching for closely related products can alert trolls and copycats and make you vulnerable to external influences and threats. It is best to be vague about your searches and research into other markets and similar products.

I was once asked to advise a group of people who had come up with a very good idea; it was electronically based, but it would have been easy enough to make a prototype. They were very eager to gather all the parts needed to build the first iteration. I asked them to take a small step backward and build the basics of the project plan, including timelines and task lists. They also wrote their journals and reflected on them even today. Once a budget and scope had been completed, we moved into build mode. I suggested we go to a few electronics stores and buy bits and pieces from each, rather than purchase all the parts from the one supplier. That way there was little chance anyone would take stock of all the parts and figure out their idea. Don't be surprised and be under no illusion: retailers want to make more money as quickly as possible and they pay close attention to what customers purchase, especially if it is an odd grouping of small items. Everyone wants to accelerate his or her earning potential; as you can see, I encourage it. However, do not allow your ideas and innovations to be reverse engineered too quickly.

Cutting through the red tape to get answers as fast as possible is a difficult but an important skill to learn. One reason I don't think many others will firmly grasp your conceptual ideas initially is because what is clear in your mind will be foggy in another's. When you try to get things done on a day-to-day basis, understand the methods of engagement to articulate your message. This is different from mind games and is more about understanding how to present information to individuals inside your target market. To develop these skills, ask yourself "what is the outcome I want from this engagement?" For example, you will need an internal champion inside the target business to help you, particularly when you attempt to sell into larger retail and distribution houses. This person on the inside can help you present the information in a way that makes his or her life easier and the target organization more comfortable with the content and layout.

Once you identify and connect with a champion, you are a long way through the process. There are two options for business tools in this area: the Internet (discussed above) or a mentor who has gone through the process in the past. Even someone who failed will be a great resource. A mentor can be from a previous organization or simply another innovator to whom you have reached out. Generally, successful innovators will be more than happy to give up a little of their time to chat about their experiences and the mistakes they've made. During the conversation, pick out the things that you can relate to, and use their experiences to enhance your own strengths. Gain knowledge from those around you; individuals can be business tools also. They are valuable resources who may serve as sounding boards or provide corporate guidance and everything in-between.

The world of an entrepreneur is generally slightly disjointed, mainly because we are different or misunderstood. In addition, there may not be an overwhelming abundance of knowledge regarding the field in which your idea fits. It's difficult to research a product when it has not yet been invented. If you have done your research and found little to no details on similar products, you probably felt an overwhelming feeling of relief and excitement. Of course, this is going to make original enhancements difficult and pricing models a challenge, but you shouldn't care; this is great news. Being unable to find information about an existing product similar to yours is akin to magic.

Your product may be identified as a change agent in the marketplace, and regardless of the threats from copycats in the future, keep in mind that people generally fall in love with an original product. You can always market it as "the original" If you stay on top of your game after the product launch, by the time anyone has put thought into copying your product, in your country or any other, you will have had time to gather feedback from consumers. In addition, you will have product enhancements waiting in the pipeline, making it immune from copy cats, because your new enhanced product will leapfrog over any others.

Innovators of all types will feel stress and anxiety build over time that they find difficult to expel. One of the greatest business tools—which I learned primarily from observing other people go from stressed to calm in the space of a week—is to go to the gym and expend energy.

That's correct: go to the gym. This is not generally considered a topic of interest for entrepreneurs. However, never underestimate the value of exercise. There are many different methods for releasing stress and anxiety. I head to the local gym about three times a week. It has not turned me into a supreme athlete but was a fantastic release. It has been proven that exercise creates a certain feeling of euphoria, and although it was hard to get to the gym, you will leave without regrets. When was the last time you regretted going to the gym? I have also gained equal benefits from practicing yoga. I started with the Hatha version then moved to the Bikram version. If you don't enjoy yoga, trust me it will grow on you. Don't think about yoga as an unpopular activity; it has become a mainstream tool to help men and women manage stress and increase body health demonstrably. Embrace yoga to manage your energy levels.

# Building Knowledge

This will be one of the most exhilarating and exciting stages in your journey. Your trusted resources are in place, and your journal is growing steadily. You are now in a position to add experience and wisdom to your collection of knowledge. Each of your resources will add something that could potentially enhance your product that little bit more. Extract information from them, and as foreign as it is for me to say, explore the Internet as aggressively as possible. The more knowledge you absorb at this stage, the better. Continue to innovate, listen, and learn.

I once followed an interesting concept called the "strategic bet." Imagine yourself on a boat sailing off the West Coast of the United States. What do you wish you had with you? The answer depends on the direction you are going. If you are headed north in winter, then you won't want summer clothes or a bikini. You would have packed for cold, blistery conditions, because the temperature will drop the further you head north. You'd pack heating pads for hands and feet, a couple of thick jackets, and clothing that you can layer to keep warm. Food will be tailored to the environment you are heading toward, as will the navigation equipment. The situation changes if your boat is traveling south. You most likely will pack lighter clothes, swimsuits, sunscreen, and towels. It's a warmer climate, and you will no doubt encounter more people than you would in a cold region.

Using this analogy, you can identify the key resources you'll need at the next stage of product production. Simply remain aware of the direction in which you are headed. Once you have made your strategic bet, it's time to equip yourself accordingly. Do not fall into the trap of purchasing unnecessary items along the way or carrying resources that don't match the direction in which you are traveling. Be frugal with spending money, and ensure that your financial investments match your funding capabilities. There is no point in buying swimsuits in the North just because they are heavily discounted up there.

You will see the value in building knowledge from your concept all the way through to production. Glean as much knowledge, experience, and wisdom as you can from your trusted resources. These resources have now been integrated substantially into your idea and are prepared to take it to market with you. Just because you are rapidly closing in on your launch date does not prevent you from increasing your knowledge. Let's examine the reservoirs of information that your resources possess.

Accountants can provide guidance regarding financial projections they have worked on with you. Their advice will always be about numbers. If you have followed the plan described in this book, you will have been working with your accountant for some time. It is beneficial to sit with them and digest the forecast from the beginning, see the progression to launch, and ask what they think projections will look like post-launch. Ask them about other projects they have worked on, gather information about successes and failures of others, and incorporate that information into your own strategy. Look for similarities, and focus on the strategies others have used to succeed. Discuss innovators who found ways not to succeed; their experiences may provide some insight into the deep world of invention, identify some traps to avoid, and utilize suggestions listed in this guide.

Business coaches have a good understanding of personalities, project strategies, and potential to deliver—often from an emotional point of view. Your conversation with your coach may get heated due to the effort and hard work you have invested so far. Still, your business coach should be a trusted entity by now and is likely to approach the conversation tactfully. During the many months the two of you have been talking, you should have absorbed a significant amount of knowledge. Hopefully, you include this information in your journal and reflect on it when needed. Continue to engage the business coach all the way through to product completion, and do not stop asking questions. Sometimes, the greatest tool you have in your arsenal is the ability to ask a question. By engaging continually in the "search for knowledge," you will grow day by day. When you ask your business coach a question, he or she should provide a detailed or educated answer, and you will gain new information each time. Continue to update your journal as you build knowledge.

 Your marketing company will have a plethora of information from previous marketing campaigns for other clients. The staff will have their own running success/failure catalogue, which can provide insight into ways to improve your campaign. Don't leave all the work to the marketing reps, though. Always check and measure their work, and push them to achieve the outcomes you desire. As mentioned previously, they should be able to identify what they have done well and not so well before developing a strategy to promote your product. They will have access to industry reports regarding other campaigns. Set up recurring meetings to keep them on track, and extract as much knowledge from them as possible. People generally slowdown unless they have a little push from time to time.

It may be a bit more difficult to extract knowledge from your technology partners. It depends on whether you have engaged them for a simple web design, social media presence management, or a fully enabled smart phone app. However, they will have input on how to use technology to market your product and promote your ideas. If you have hired them to design a simple website or set up your social media presence, chances are they will have introduced you to a graphic designer or a technical writer to help you make your product as attractive as possible. Ask these secondary resources to sign nondisclosure agreements and feel comfortable about their involvement. I must say that IT people enjoy having their egos stroked. If you need a quick improvement on the campaign or are mining for knowledge, remark on how good they are and that you are glad they are on board. Yes, you will be playing tiny mind games. However, it's harmless, so go for it. Gather as much knowledge as you can, and document it in your journal.

If you are in a position to do so, and you should be if you have played your cards well, ask all your resources for historical information and data that will provide insight into the success and failure of a previous campaign. Remember that you are seeking suppliers that perform and deliver; shift to another company if you feel uncomfortable. While such a move is not ideal at this stage, it is better than letting the project head toward failure. I cannot say this enough: always remember that you are not looking for a new best friend.

# The Wrap Up

There is little I can add about the execution or wrap-up phase—other than, good luck. The eve of a new product launch is a rewarding and exciting time for every entrepreneur. Your valuable resources have helped you on your journey. With the addition of the contract negotiator and relaxation brought about by exercise, you now can judge your readiness. The final stage of execution comes from within you. You have to be the driving force behind the product you've invented.

Reflect on the entries in your journal and in your project plan. Try and understand what went well and what didn't; learning from your mistakes makes you a better, stronger person. Look after your documentation, and make sure everything is backed up regularly on an external data source, ready for your next venture. Your calendar items and the structure of your task list are important. Everyone is different, and over the course of this journey, you will have found your own techniques for defining tasks and capturing information—an additional talent to add to your repertoire of skills.

Consider your notes and documentation to be living documents. They will continually evolve and change as you grow as an innovator. Keep them updated, because they are something that most people dream about—a documented, step-by-step guide to guaranteed success. It is important to note, however, that you cannot transfer this knowledge of understanding to others. It is your recipe book for success—tailored for you by you.

Your strategy and resource group are malleable and will shift over time, depending on the direction of your current project and future innovations. Allow for change, but ensure you are not making a knee-jerk reaction. Stick to the plan you have created and move gently when confronted by external events that influence your project. Stay true to your plan, but allow minor shifts as part of the growth strategy for your projects and yourself.

Respect your customer base. It is difficult to market to the consumer; manage expectations, and be consistent about your message. If your product is a repetitive sell, consumers generally continue to purchase simply because they enjoy it and are creatures of habit. Since the days of the cavemen days, repetitive actions have been an inherent human characteristic. If your product is a one-time purchase for long-term purposes, your customers are equally important. Word of mouth, positive feedback, and press releases promoting your product are your greatest and most cost-effective marketing approaches. Respect the positive feedback, respect the negative feedback, and discard the trolls.

You have a huge advantage with your first product launch. You will be perceived as a new player in which ever vertical your product fits. As a newbie, you will have more demands on your business than others with long-time solutions. Competitors generally do not see your ability to have a smaller operation and be as nimble as you can as a threat, and it enables you to move faster, respond more quickly, and remain on top of your game. Even if you decide to step back and gather your thoughts, or to reflect on how to improve your product, it will be hardly noticeable. Just don't disappear for too long.

In this wrap-up chapter, I wanted to touch on the two major strategies entrepreneurs use when launching anything new: a *soft launch* and a *hard launch*.

A soft launch is a targeted marking campaign to a selected community of buyers to gauge their spending trends and feedback. Choose a small group from a demographic that matches the characteristics of your broader consumer base and market directly to that group. Document the results as they come in; they will enable you to tailor your strategy for a hard launch.

A hard launch promotes your product to your entire target customer base, using everything in your marketing arsenal. The goal is to capture as many sales as possible. Use the information you have gathered from the soft launch to make slight adjustments to your campaign, based on feedback obtained, sales made, and indications of buying trends. Some entrepreneurs move straight to the hard launch. However, it is highly intelligent to test your target market via a soft launch to further tailor your campaign. Without good information, it is difficult to make great business decisions. Believe in the mantra that information is power.

 Your hard work and dedication up to this point have been just the tip of the iceberg. I'm happy to say that there is more work to be done. Don't worry too much, though; by now, you should have allocated the critical tasks to the correct resources. Financial management belongs with your accountant; changes to product specifications belong to your patent lawyer; and everything else can be covered by the other trusted resources. You just need to remain informed about all aspects of the project and continue to influence the outcomes. It is your product, so do not become complacent. Even your trusted resources must be kept focused, held accountable, and rewarded for all their contributions.

Never become disconnected or have self-doubt regarding negative feedback. Take it on board, and if required, alter your strategy. Many consumers will complain about something regarding your product from time to time, as they do about all products. Do not under any circumstances lose direction or become sad; sadness is a virus that can easily consume your thoughts and slow or even stop your successes. I have seen it happen to people I have mentored. No matter how motivating

I can be, a loss of vision is such a slippery slope, it is difficult to climb back up. The second you start doubting blaming yourself for anything that happened during the launch, it makes it tougher. So, let's decide not to! What do you think?

Below are summaries of the key points in each chapter.

## Don't Be Afraid

Learn from those around you how to manage your emotions better, and do not allow others to project their fear and anxiety onto you. If you are consumed by fear, your project will take longer to complete. Only one person can control how you feel, and that's you. You are in control of every aspect of your life. Sometimes I go for long walks to clear my head. I also am fond of the gym; exercising reduces stress and anxiety. Exercise a few times a week, and allow your idea to grow organically in the background.

## What Is an Entrepreneur?

There will always be two sides to the entrepreneur's personality. As with everything in life, there are always extremes and a balanced middle ground. If you are an innovator entrepreneur, then your goal will be to brush up on the basics of business management and gain knowledge in areas outside your normal comfort zone. If you are a business entrepreneur, get in touch with your purely creative and hands-on side; perhaps design something using equipment bought at the hardware store. Do something to make sure you don't lose touch with the other side of yourself. If entrepreneurs get this piece right, they will slowly move toward the middle of the spectrum, where true balanced creativity can happen.

## Different or Misunderstood

Most people will have different opinions about your character and personality and will try to work out where you fit in their eco-system. That's reality. If they are narcissists or high-earning sales executives or have an aggressive business persona, they will have a mantra to determine if you are with them or if you are against them, which is all they will care about. They will think, *What have you done for me lately?* to determine if they want you on their team. These people and several more may see you as "different." Professional managers and potential business partners will see through all the confusion and will think you are simply "misunderstood." The group of people who can see that you fit under both descriptions may be the right people to associate with, when the time is right.

## Start by Trusting No One

Trust no one with your ideas or your strategy for the future; just vet the potentials. Try to subdue that burning desire to shout out your idea to anyone who will listen; it will be gone in a flash. The success of your idea lies heavily on your ability to keep everything to yourself at this stage. Work on your documentation and project plan, and keep your journal up-to-date. Rely on your tools to help you through this phase.

## Move to Trusting Someone

When you have a stable grip on your idea, and clarity around the resources you'll need to make it happen, move to lightly trusting someone. Engage the resources you have researched in order to progress to the next stage. Stay with the independent group you have identified and away from engaging family or friends to join the journey. Once you have gathered your consortium, hand out only a small amount of trust at first; let the resources know that they have to earn the rest of your trust if they want to continue working with you. Finally, don't share your ideas with people simply because they seem nice. They won't be too nice about sharing profits with you if they beat you to the finish line.

Your trusted group will be key to your success for two primary reasons. These people will provide support and encouragement and highlight potential pitfalls. Strive to achieve balance; surrounding yourself with "yes" men or women will set you up for failure. Each member of your group will have a distinct set of skills. Each will bring his or her own unique value to the project. Be prepared for the possibility that you may not get along from time to time, but remember a common goal always unites a team.

All entrepreneurs increase their potential to succeed when they surround themselves with good people; anyone who has achieved greatness will tell you this is true. Remember that these people are there to help you as an individual—and not the product—succeed. This may be hard to get your head around, but when you reach this stage you will understand. If all goes well, these people could be with you for many projects to come. Take care of them, encourage them to take care of each other, and they will in turn look out for you.

## Expect Resistance

Resistance to your idea and project will come thick and fast. It takes time to become part of a process. Steel your emotions to help you ignore the resistance until it subsides. It may never go away entirely. For example, if you successfully keep narcissists outside your inner circle, they will resist in any way possible. Investors use resistance techniques to drive down the owner's equity and increase their own shares, as far as you allow them. Their goal is to ensure that their return on investment is as high and accelerated as possible. Remain strong, and be prepared to walk away from the deal if there is an imbalance between the investment and your equity. There are many investors out there looking to invest in promising new products, especially if they are new to the marketplace. You will hit resistance until the deal is signed; then investors often will contribute their own skills to the project to protect their investment. Remember that old saying: "An investor is like a hitchhiker; everything will be smooth sailing if you are taking them in the direction they want to go. The second you deviate from that course, they will knock you over the head and steal your wallet." Investors are not a trusted resources until they prove themselves to be so.

Consumers are one group who will resist you from day one and never really stop. They will look for cheaper deals and resist paying the recommended retail price, because we live in a society where people need to feel they have won. The moment you play around with promotions and alter pricing structures, that will become the reality. The consumer will provide more resistance if you then take away the price drop and promotion. Shopping and buying is a sport for most people.

## Mind Games

Mind games are played at many different levels—from mostly harmless to the games a narcissist would play. Do not get too involved in the mind games played by others. Instead, identify the bulldog who will help you along the way, a great asset for keeping things moving and removing obstacles. An important skill to master is to remain mindful, which is often hard. However, we need mindfulness if we are to succeed. Skills and assistance from trusted resources will be critical to helping you navigate the mine field of difficulties that you will face. Face them confidently.

## Beware of the Narcissist

A narcissist is a one-person wrecking machine. Narcissists truly believe they are always right. They generally don't have any genuine friends. While working to destroy others and build their own pathetic egos, they will eventually self-destruct. When their narcissism is discovered by too many people, they fade into the background and target someone else in a different vertical. Trust me; if you follow this guide and pay attention, you can avoid this part of the journey.

## Business Tools

Choose your tools well, and do not overcomplicate things. Task management applications work well for any smart device. Obtain one that allows you to set due dates and leave notes; this is a way of documenting your progress. Project management applications are readily available; look for one that is easy to use but has the high-level ability to capture large portions of your project. Then use your task management program to drill down.

Post zero information on social media until the time is right. The social media landscape is difficult to master and highly volatile, but it does have a purpose. In our case, it is to grow sales and awareness of your product. However, use social media with extreme caution. It is not a forum for idle chit-chat; once information is in the public medium, it's there for all to see and exploit, most likely forever. But there is a place for social media when you are promoting your idea.

## Building Knowledge

As the old saying goes, knowledge is power. Your awareness and holistic view of innovation grows significantly as you progress from idea to production. As you will document the journey, you will identify areas where you lack experience. Your trusted resources will help you prepare for a successful launch. At this stage of the project, you will have ample opportunity and awareness to conduct some research on marketing your product, identifying similar products already in the marketplace, determining how competitors market their products, and confidently finding your place in the overall pecking order. The Internet, when used correctly, is a great place to build knowledge; for example, you can see what others are doing on social media and review credible websites. Hopefully, I won't need to remind you to document these findings.

## The Wrap Up

Finally, congratulate yourself regularly on your journey— both for your progress and for what you have learned about yourself. Maintain the great connections with your trusted resources, and the methods you used to identify and engage them. They were a large part of your journey and a launch party is probably on the cards. If you have gone through the steps in this book and continued through your journey of innovation—knowing that 96 percent of the population does not have the courage, determination, or strength to join the elite group of entrepreneurs who make the world a better place—you are way ahead of the pack.

Welcome aboard. Enjoy being an entrepreneur!

Printed in the United States
By Bookmasters